YOUR

EXTRAORDINARY

LIFE
Journal

AND BIBLE READING PLAN

YOUR EXTRAORDINARY LIFE Journal
AND BIBLE READING PLAN

ISBN: 978-1-61718-010-1

intendresources.com

Our prayer is for the body of believers in the Earth—
spotless through faith, made in His image and carrying
the Name of His Son.

May you live every day in the full knowledge of the truth
that God has created you to be His advocate in this time,
and to do the good works He prepared for you.

Chronological Bible Reading Plan

This year, read the Bible in the order the stories actually occurred. Just check off each day as you finish the reading to keep up. If you would like a Bible organized in a daily fashion using this chart, visit intendministries.org/dailyreading

- ☐ Day 1: Gen 1-3
- ☐ Day 2: Gen 4-7
- ☐ Day 3: Gen 8-11
- ☐ Day 4: Job 1-5
- ☐ Day 5: Job 6-10
- ☐ Day 6: Job 11-14
- ☐ Day 7: Job 15-17
- ☐ Day 8: Job 18-20
- ☐ Day 9: Job 21-25
- ☐ Day 10: Job 26-28
- ☐ Day 11: Job 29-31
- ☐ Day 12: Job 32-34
- ☐ Day 13: Job 35-37
- ☐ Day 14: Job 38-39
- ☐ Day 15: Job 40-42
- ☐ Day 16: Gen 12-15
- ☐ Day 17: Gen 16-18:15
- ☐ Day 18: Gen 18:16-21
- ☐ Day 19: Gen 22-24
- ☐ Day 20: Gen 25-26
- ☐ Day 21: Gen 27-29
- ☐ Day 22: Gen 30-31
- ☐ Day 23: Gen 32-34
- ☐ Day 24: Gen 35-37
- ☐ Day 25: Gen 38-40
- ☐ Day 26: Gen 41-42
- ☐ Day 27: Gen 43-45
- ☐ Day 28: Gen 46-47
- ☐ Day 29: Gen 48-50
- ☐ Day 30: Ex 1-3
- ☐ Day 31: Ex 4-6
- ☐ Day 32: Ex 7-9
- ☐ Day 33: Ex 10-12
- ☐ Day 34: Ex 13-15
- ☐ Day 35: Ex 16-18
- ☐ Day 36: Ex 19-21
- ☐ Day 37: Ex 22-24
- ☐ Day 38: Ex 25-27
- ☐ Day 39: Ex 28-29
- ☐ Day 40: Ex 30-31
- ☐ Day 41: Ex 32-34
- ☐ Day 42: Ex 35-37
- ☐ Day 43: Ex 38-40
- ☐ Day 44: Lev 1-4
- ☐ Day 45: Lev 5-7
- ☐ Day 46: Lev 8-10
- ☐ Day 47: Lev 11-13
- ☐ Day 48: Lev 14-15
- ☐ Day 49: Lev 16-18
- ☐ Day 50: Lev 19-21
- ☐ Day 51: Lev 22-23
- ☐ Day 52: Lev 24-25
- ☐ Day 53: Lev 26-27
- ☐ Day 54: Num 1-2
- ☐ Day 55: Num 3-4
- ☐ Day 56: Num 5-6
- ☐ Day 57: Num 7
- ☐ Day 58: Num 8-10
- ☐ Day 59: Num 11-13
- ☐ Day 60: Num 14-15; Ps 90
- ☐ Day 61: Num 16-17
- ☐ Day 62: Num 18-20
- ☐ Day 63: Num 21-22
- ☐ Day 64: Num 23-25
- ☐ Day 65: Num 26-27
- ☐ Day 66: Num 28-30
- ☐ Day 67: Num 31-32
- ☐ Day 68: Num 33-34
- ☐ Day 69: Num 35-36
- ☐ Day 70: Deut 1-2

- ☐ Day 71: Deut 3-4
- ☐ Day 72: Deut 5-7
- ☐ Day 73: Deut 8-10
- ☐ Day 74: Deut 11-13
- ☐ Day 75: Deut 14-16
- ☐ Day 76: Deut 17-20
- ☐ Day 77: Deut 21-23
- ☐ Day 78: Deut 24-27
- ☐ Day 79: Deut 28-29
- ☐ Day 80: Deut 30-31
- ☐ Day 81: Deut 32-34; Ps 91
- ☐ Day 82: Josh 1-4
- ☐ Day 83: Josh 5-8
- ☐ Day 84: Josh 9-11
- ☐ Day 85: Josh 12-15
- ☐ Day 86: Josh 16-18
- ☐ Day 87: Josh 19-21
- ☐ Day 88: Josh 22-24
- ☐ Day 89: Jud 1-2
- ☐ Day 90: Jud 3-5
- ☐ Day 91: Jud 6-7
- ☐ Day 92: Jud 8-9
- ☐ Day 93: Jud 10-12
- ☐ Day 94: Jud 13-15
- ☐ Day 95: Jud 16-18
- ☐ Day 96: Jud 19-21
- ☐ Day 97: Ruth
- ☐ Day 98: 1Sam 1-3
- ☐ Day 99: 1Sam 4-7
- ☐ Day 100: 1Sam 8-10
- ☐ Day 101: 1Sam 11-13:22
- ☐ Day 102: 1Sam 13:23-17
- ☐ Day 103: 1Sam 10-20; Ps 11/59
- ☐ Day 104: 1Sam 21-24
- ☐ Day 105: Ps 7/27/31/34/52
- ☐ Day 106: Ps 56/120/140-142
- ☐ Day 107: 1Sam 25-27
- ☐ Day 108: Ps 17/35/54/63
- ☐ Day 109: 1Sam 28-31; Ps18
- ☐ Day 110: Ps 121 Ps 123-125/128-130
- ☐ Day 111: 2Sam 1-4
- ☐ Day 112: Ps 6/8-10 Ps 14/16/19/21
- ☐ Day 113: 1Chron 1-2
- ☐ Day 114: Ps 43-45/49 Ps 84-85/87
- ☐ Day 115: 1Chron 3-5
- ☐ Day 116: Ps 73/77-78
- ☐ Day 117: 1Chron 6
- ☐ Day 118: Ps 81/88/92-93
- ☐ Day 119: 1Chron 7-10
- ☐ Day 120: Ps 102-104
- ☐ Day 121: 2Sam 5:1-10; 1Chron 11-12; Ps 133
- ☐ Day 122: Ps 106-107; 2 Sam 5-6
- ☐ Day 123: 1Chron 13-16
- ☐ Day 124: Ps 1-2/15/22-24
- ☐ Day 125: Ps 47/68/89
- ☐ Day 126: 96/100-101/105/132
- ☐ Day 127: 2Sam 7; 1Chron 17
- ☐ Day 128: Ps 25/29/33/36/39
- ☐ Day 129: 2Sam 8-9; 1Chron 18
- ☐ Day 130: Ps 50/53/60/75
- ☐ Day 131: 2Sam10; 1Chron 19; Ps 20
- ☐ Day 132: Ps 65-67/69-70
- ☐ Day 133: 2Sam 11-12; 1Chron 20
- ☐ Day 134: Ps 32/51/86/122
- ☐ Day 135: 2Sam 13-15
- ☐ Day 136: Ps 3-4/12-13/28/55
- ☐ Day 137: 2Sam 16-18
- ☐ Day 138: Ps 26/40/58 Ps 61-62/64
- ☐ Day 139: 2Sam 19-21
- ☐ Day 140: Ps 5/38/41-42
- ☐ Day 141: 2Sam 22-23; Ps 57
- ☐ Day 142: Ps 95/97-99
- ☐ Day 143: 2Sam 24; 1Chron 21-22; Ps 30
- ☐ Day 144: Ps 108-110
- ☐ Day 145: 1Chron 23-25

YOUR

EXTRAORDINARY

LIFE
Journal

Be joyful in hope, patient in affliction, faithful in prayer.
(Romans 12:12)

*Hear me, LORD, my plea is just; listen to my cry. Hear my prayer —
it does not rise from deceitful lips.* (Psalm 17:1)

Praise be to God, who has not rejected my prayer or withheld his love from me! (Psalm 66:20)

If you believe, you will receive whatever you ask for in prayer.
(Matthew 21:22)

Praise awaits you, our God, in Zion;
to you our vows will be fulfilled. (Psalm 65:1)

But I cry to you for help, LORD; in the morning my prayer comes before you. (Psalm 88:13)

The LORD is far from the wicked, but he hears the prayer of the righteous. (Proverbs 15:29)

WORLD OUTREACH CHURCH

40

Devote yourselves to prayer, being watchful and thankful.
(Colossians 4:2)

Therefore I tell you, whatever you ask for in prayer, believe that you have received it, and it will be yours. (Mark 11:24)

When my life was ebbing away, I remembered you, LORD, and my prayer rose to you, to your holy temple. (Jonah 2:7)

...in every situation, by prayer and petition, with thanksgiving, present your requests to God. (Philippians 4:6)

He will respond to the prayer of the destitute; he will not despise their plea. (Psalm 102:17)

*So we fasted and petitioned our God about this,
and he answered our prayer. (Ezra 8:23)*

And this is my prayer: that your love may abound more and more in knowledge and depth of insight (Philippians 1:9)

YOUR EXTRAORDINARY LIFE

The prayer of a righteous person is powerful and effective. (James 5:16)

69

And the prayer offered in faith will make the sick person well; the Lord will raise them up. (James 5:15)

You are my strength, I watch for you; you, God, are my fortress
(Psalm 59:9)

The LORD is my strength and my defense; he has become my salvation. (Psalm 118:14)

He gives strength to the weary and increases the power of the weak.
(Isaiah 40:29)

But you, LORD, do not be far from me. You are my strength; come quickly to help me. (Psalm 22:19)

*My flesh and my heart may fail, but God is the strength of my heart
and my portion forever. (Psalm 73:26)*

Praise the LORD. Praise God in his sanctuary; praise him in his mighty heavens. (Psalm 150:1)

My mouth will speak in praise of the LORD. Let every creature praise his holy name for ever and ever. (Psalm 145:21)

Praise be to the LORD, the God of Israel, from everlasting to everlasting. (1 Chronicles 16:36)

*I have chosen the way of faithfulness; I have set
my heart on your laws. (Psalm 119:30)*

Righteousness and justice are the foundation of your throne; love and faithfulness go before you. (Psalm 89:14)

But you, Lord, are a compassionate and gracious God, slow to anger, abounding in love and faithfulness. (Psalm 86:15)

Yet you desired faithfulness even in the womb; you taught me wisdom in that secret place. (Psalm 51:6)

Your love, LORD, reaches to the heavens, your faithfulness to the skies. (Psalm 36:5)

Light shines on the righteous and joy on the upright in heart.
(Psalm 97:11)

Your statutes are my heritage forever; they are the joy of my heart.
(Psalm 119:111)

My lips will shout for joy when I sing praise to you—
I whom you have delivered. (Psalm 71:23)

The prospect of the righteous is joy, but the hopes of the wicked come to nothing. (Proverbs 10:28)

With joy you will draw water from the wells of salvation.
(Isaiah 12:3)

You turned my wailing into dancing; you removed my sackcloth and clothed me with joy (Psalm 30:11)

When anxiety was great within me, your consolation brought me joy.
(Psalm 94:19)

There is no fear in love. But perfect love drives out fear
(1 John 4:18)

And now these three remain : faith, hope and love.
But the greatest of these is love. (1 Corinthians 13:13)

Now, my God, may your eyes be open and your ears attentive to the prayers offered in this place. (2 Chronicles 6:40)

Pray for the peace of Jerusalem: May those who love you be secure.
(Psalm 122:6)

LORD my God, I take refuge in you;
save and deliver me from all who pursue me (Psalm 7:1)

I say to the LORD, "You are my Lord;
apart from you I have no good thing." (Psalm 16:2)

I call on you, my God, for you will answer me
(Psalm 17:6)

He guides me along the right paths for his name's sake.
(Psalm 23:3)

INTEND RESOURCES

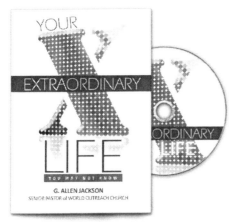

Order Pastor G. Allen Jackson's sermon series entitled "Your Extraordinary Life", available on both CD and DVD.

Freedom from Worry is a book by G. Allen Jackson that applies Biblical truth to bring new hope to those struggling with anxiety and unbelief.

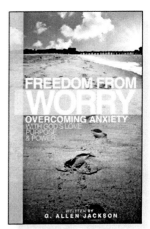

To order these and other resources from Intend,
visit **intendresources.com**

World Outreach Church

World Outreach Church is an interdenominational Christian Church in the mainstream of the historic Christian faith. The Apostle's Creed frames our statement of belief. We have experienced many changes through the years, but one set of values has remained the same--our desire to experience God more fully in our lives; the belief that a relationship with Jesus Christ is transforming; a commitment to children and young people; and a desire to be a valuable participant in our community.

Pastor G. Allen Jackson